# SOUTH COAST RAILWAYS —

# RYDE

## TO

# VENTNOR

## Vic Mitchell and Keith Smith

*Design – Deborah Goodridge*

*First published 1985*
*Revised and reprinted 1987*

*ISBN 0 906520 19 3*

*© Middleton Press, 1987*

*Typeset by CitySet - Bosham 573270*

*Published by Middleton Press*
           *Easebourne Lane*
           *Midhurst, West Sussex*
           *GU29 9AZ*
           *☎ 073 081 3169*

*Printed & bound by Biddles Ltd,*
           *Guildford and Kings Lynn*

# CONTENTS

# ACKNOWLEDGEMENTS

Our grateful thanks go to all those mentioned in the captions not only for providing prints or loaning photographs but also for help with information in many cases. Thanks also go to N. Langridge for the loan of tickets; to H. Hunt for help with ferry timetables; to Miss S. Maine for use of her passenger survey; to R. Randall for research assistance; to Mrs. E. Fisk and N. Stanyon for proof reading and to our ever helpful wives.

# AUTHOR'S NOTES

Over fifteen different books have been published on the Isle of Wight railways and details of the locomotives, rolling stock and many of the staff have been fully recorded. We do not intend to repeat this information but prefer to attempt to recreate in words and pictures the unique atmosphere of the best known line and also to portray fully the sleepy Bembridge branch.

The majority of photographs have not been previously published; the few that have are included because we have found better prints which can be enjoyed to the full when reproduced in enlarged form. We have chosen semi-matt paper which gives the same detail in the pictures without reflected lights spoiling the viewing – just as art galleries use non-reflective glass over fine paintings.

We plan to produce another album to cover other Island lines and would be pleased to hear from anyone with any unusual and unpublished views.

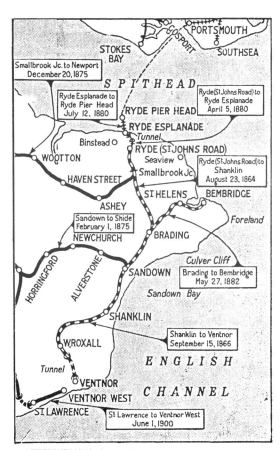

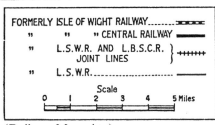

(Railway Magazine)

# GEOGRAPHICAL SETTING

The varied geology can be easily seen in the cliffs at the east and west ends of the island, since the strata lie on that axis. As the railway route is at right angles to them, all the different strata are crossed which results in very varied terrain and flora, similar to the Petersfield to Havant and Midhurst to Chichester lines.

From Ryde the railway crosses the undulating northern plain, composed of marls and gravels and at Brading it joins the valley of the tiny River Yar, which passes through a gap in the Downs that form the spine of the Island. It is similar to the gap in the South Downs at Arundel, used by the Mid-Sussex line.

The Sandown area is, not surprisingly, a region of fairly level sand, which continues to Shanklin. Thereafter, the line climbed steeply through sandrock and crossed an area of gault clay at Wroxall before penetrating the chalk mass of South Wight to reach Ventnor. The railway builders had considered avoiding tunnelling by taking their line along the cliffs, but dramatic landslips here have subsequently proved their judgement to be prudent.

## HISTORICAL BACKGROUND

The main line of what was to become known as the Isle of Wight Railway was opened between Ryde and Shanklin in 1864, being extended to Ventnor in 1866. The Ryde terminus was on the southern fringe of the town, about a mile from the pier head. A horse-operated tramway ran on the pier and was eventually extended along the shore and southwards to the railway terminus. This connection frustrated through passengers for many years and Island authorities seemed unable to resolve the problem.

The London & South Western Railway and the London Brighton & South Coast Railway had formed a joint Committee to operate the railways into Portsmouth, for reasons explained in our companion album *Chichester to Portsmouth*. These mainland companies saw the Ryde bottleneck restricting the development of tourism on the Island and in consequence their potential traffic. They therefore took the matter into their own hands and obtained an Act of Parliament to construct a double track railway on a new pier; to tunnel under the sea front highway (so precious to the inhabitants) and to join up with the existing lines at St. John's Road. The local companies would operate their own trains on the Joint Committee's lines, which were eventualy opened to traffic on 5th April 1880.

In 1875 the Isle of Wight Central Railway started services from Newport to Sandown and to Ryde. The IWR provided a single track parallel to their own for the last mile of the journey to St. John's Road. The precise dates of opening are shown on the accompanying map, reproduced by kind permission of the editor of the Railway Magazine.

Little changed until 1923, when all the lines became part of the newly formed Southern Railway. To meet the increased demands of tourism, the SR doubled the line between Brading and Sandown, also arranging for the two single lines south of Ryde to be worked as double track when necessary. Other improvements are described elsewhere in this album.

With the formation of British Railways in 1948, there were few changes, other than in livery – even the engines retained their old names and numbers. The Beeching Plan envisaged closure of all the Island's railways but, for once, vigorous protest was largely successful and the Ryde to Shanklin section survived. The southern extremity, however, unfortunately lost its service on 18th April 1966. The remaining line was closed between January and March 1967, to allow for the completion of third-rail electrification and the raising of the track in stations to permit the operation of second-hand London Under-

Bradshaw 1869

Gen. Man., Joseph Bourne, Ryde.] ISLE OF WIGHT. [Sec., R. Hicks.

| Fares. Single. 1 cl. | 2 cl. | 3 cl. | Return. 1 cl. | 2 cl. | 3 cl. | Down. | Week Days. 1,2,3 | 1&2 | 1&2 | 1&2 | 1&2 | 1&2 | 1&2 | 1&2 | 1&2 | 1&2 | 1&2 | 1&2 | Sundays. 1,2,3 | 1&2 | 1&2 |
|---|---|---|---|---|---|---|---|---|---|---|---|---|---|---|---|---|---|---|---|---|---|
| | | | | | | Ryde......dep | 7 20 | 8 20 | 9 30 | 1025 | 1125 | 1250 | 2 30 | 3 30 | 5 15 | 6 15 | 7 20 | 8 15 | 9 25 | 3 0 | 7 30 |
| 0 10 | 0 6 | 0 3½ | 1 3 | 0 9 | 0 7 | Brading ...... | 7 29 | 8 29 | 9 38 | 1033 | 1133 | 1259 | 2 39 | 3 39 | 5 24 | 6 23 | 7 29 | 8 24 | 9 34 | 3 9 | 7 39 |
| 1 3 | 0 9 | 0 5½ | 1 11 | 1 2 | 0 11 | Sandown...... | 7 36 | 8 36 | 9 44 | 1039 | 1139 | 1 6 | 2 46 | 3 46 | 5 31 | 6 28 | 7 36 | 8 31 | 9 41 | 3 16 | 7 46 |
| 1 8 | 1 0 | 0 7 | 2 6 | 1 6 | 1 2 | Shanklin .... | 7 43 | 8 43 | 9 50 | 1045 | 1145 | 1 13 | 2 53 | 3 53 | 5 38 | 6 36 | 7 43 | 8 38 | 9 48 | 3 23 | 7 53 |
| 2 3 | 1 5 | 0 10½ | 3 5 | 2 2 | 1 9 | Wroxall ...... | 7 50 | 8 50 | 9 56 | 1051 | 1151 | 1 20 | 3 0 | 4 0 | 5 45 | 6 43 | 7 50 | 8 45 | 9 55 | 3 30 | 8 0 |
| 2 8 | 1 8 | 0 11½ | 4 0 | 2 6 | 1 11 | Ventnor 1 arr | 7 57 | 8 57 | 10 2 | 1057 | 1157 | 1 27 | 3 7 | 4 7 | 5 52 | 6 50 | 7 57 | 8 52 | 10 2 | 3 37 | 8 7 |

| Single. 1 cl. | 2 cl. | 3 cl. | Return. 1 cl. | 2 cl. | 3 cl. | Up. | 1,2,3 | 1&2 | 1&2 | 1&2 | 1&2 | 1&2 | 1&2 | 1&2 | 1&2 | 1&2 | 1&2 | 1&2 | 1,2,3 | 1&2 | 1&2 |
|---|---|---|---|---|---|---|---|---|---|---|---|---|---|---|---|---|---|---|---|---|---|
| | | | | | | Ventnor ..dep | 8 15 | 9 25 | 1020 | 1157 | 1245 | 2 25 | 4 25 | 5 10 | 6 10 | 7 15 | 8 10 | 8 55 | 1010 | 3 45 | 8 15 |
| 0 4 | 0 3 | 0 1½ | 0 6 | 0 5 | 0 3 | Wroxall ...... | 8 22 | 9 31 | 1026 | 12 3 | 1252 | 2 32 | 4 32 | 5 17 | 6 17 | 7 22 | 8 17 | 9 2 | 1017 | 3 53 | 8 22 |
| 1 0 | 0 8 | 0 4 | 1 6 | 1 0 | 0 8 | Shanklin .... | 8 29 | 9 38 | 1033 | 12 9 | 1259 | 2 39 | 4 39 | 5 24 | 6 23 | 7 29 | 8 24 | 9 9 | 1024 | 3 59 | 8 29 |
| 1 4 | 0 10 | 0 6 | 2 0 | 1 3 | 1 0 | Sandown...... | 8 36 | 9 44 | 1039 | 1215 | 1 6 | 2 46 | 4 46 | 5 31 | 6 29 | 7 36 | 8 31 | 9 16 | 1031 | 4 6 | 8 36 |
| 1 10 | 1 2 | 0 7 | 2 9 | 1 9 | 1 2 | Brading ..[52 | 8 43 | 9 50 | 1045 | 1221 | 1 13 | 2 53 | 4 53 | 5 38 | 6 35 | 7 43 | 8 38 | 9 23 | 1038 | 4 13 | 8 43 |
| 2 8 | 1 8 | 0 11½ | 4 6 | 2 6 | 1 11 | Ryde34,35,38 | 8 52 | 9 58 | 1053 | 1229 | 1 22 | 3 2 | 5 2 | 5 46 | 6 43 | 7 52 | 8 47 | 9 31 | 1047 | 4 22 | 8 52 |

1, Station for Blackgang, Niton, and Freshwater.
☞ 3rd class Return Tickets issued by 7 20 mrn. Down, and 8 15 mrn. Up, are available to return by 12 45 and 6 10 aft. Up, and 12 50 and 6¼ aft. Down.

ground tube trains. Before that, the Island had become a Mecca for steam enthusiasts, being one of the last outposts of steam on BR. Twenty years on, the antiquated electrics, spurned by steam lovers, now have their own admirers, although the inadequate heaters and wide-open doors do not endear them to Islanders in mid-winter.

* * * * *

The branch from Brading to Bembridge was built by the Brading Harbour and Railway Co. and opened to passengers on 27th May 1882. The trains were operated by the IWR, who took over the company in 1898. The harbour and railway were inseparable, so that BR found itself still operating a toll road across the old harbour mouth, years after the last train had run on 21st September 1953. Both stations were sited at the bottom of hills, some distance from the village centres, which gave the competitive buses an advantage.

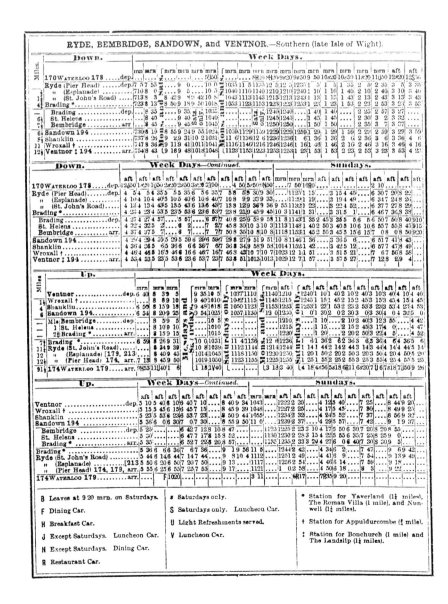

RYDE, BEMBRIDGE, SANDOWN, and VENTNOR.—Southern (late Isle of Wight).

# PASSENGER SERVICES

→

The initial weekday timetable provided for seven return journeys, which was increased to twelve for the following summer. The coach connection to Ventnor ran four times a day and added an hour to the journey time.

In 1893, a non-stop train, *The Invalid Express*, from Pier Head to Ventnor was introduced. It had a 21-minute schedule and was intended for the use of patients of the Sanatorium (which principally treated tuberculosis, then known as consumption). The normal schedule was around 40 minutes.

By 1925, there were up to 26 trains per day in the summer which was increased to three per hour in 1930. The fastest recorded run was on the 6.30 am from Ventnor one morning in 1931 when it succeeded in reaching Pier Head in 28 minutes 6 seconds having stopped (briefly) at all stations and reached 56½ mph at Smallbrook Junction.

The summer Saturday service in 1933 from Ryde Pier Head had, each hour, a non-stop to Ventnor; two trains that were first stop Brading and one stopping at all stations to Shanklin only. The following year the east-west service was extended to Ventnor, starting from there at about 10 am and giving a through train to Freshwater named *The Tourist*.

In the summer of 1936, there were 38 trains daily to Ventnor with an extra 8 to Sandown and 1 to Shanklin. The corresponding figures for 1952 were 28, 9 and 9. In the meantime, a service during World War II was maintained, an important traffic being essential workers to and from the factories at Cowes.

The 1964 timetable offered an hourly service during the winter with two per hour in the summer, augmented by nine extra trips to Shanklin and four to Sandown on Saturdays. Thus this unique line could appear to be a tranquil branch line in the off season and more like a bustling suburban steam railway of fifty years earlier in the peak season.

Undoubtedly electrification brought into being the best service ever, with a basic 30-minute interval, peaking to five trains per

1. Steam ships started operating regularly between Ryde and Portsmouth in 1825 and continued to do so until 1969. No visit to the railways of the Garden Island is complete without a look at a ferry, as this route was railway controlled from 1880 until 1984. It is unfortunate that many through booking facilities were withdrawn in March 1985, a very retrograde step. The 825-ton *P.S. Whippingham* was built in 1930 and is seen here on its last day in service, 1st September 1962. (A.E. Bennett)

_____

hour on summer Saturdays. During the mid-1970s the latter was reduced to four and eventually to 20 minute intervals.

\* \* \* \* \*

The Bembridge branch service has always connected with almost all main line trains that stopped at Brading. Thus before World War II there were about a dozen return trips on the branch and this was increased to 25 after the SR improvements took full effect, right up until the closure of the line.

## THE FUTURE

A passenger survey in 1983 showed that 68% of passengers had arrived in Portsmouth by train; 40% would re-visit the Island if its trains were steam hauled and over 20% had decided to visit one of the resorts because they could complete the journey by rail. With the current trend towards privatisation, maybe the day will come when steam will reappear at the Pier Head. If steam trains only ran in the evenings, when the current could be switched off, it could give a massive boost to the hotel trade. Of the 350 or so steam locomotives preserved in the UK, there are many of suitable size and power that are under utilised or with nowhere suitable to run.

1884 steamer services

## STEAM PACKET SERVICE TO RYDE AND COWES—WEEK DAYS.

| | a.m. | a.m. | a.m. | a.m. | a.m. | a.m. | noon | p.m. | p.m. | p.m. | p.m. | p.m. | p.m. | p.m. | p.m. | p.m. | p.m. | p.m. | p.m. |
|---|---|---|---|---|---|---|---|---|---|---|---|---|---|---|---|---|---|---|---|
| tsmth (rbr. Pr.) dep. | ... | 8 10 | 7 40 | 9 10 | 9 45 | 10 55 | 12 10 | 12 10 | 1 20 | ... | 2 0 | 2 30 | 2 20 | 3 50 | 4 30 | 4 40 | ... | 5 55 | 6 45 | ... | ... | ... | ... | ... | ... |
| thsea ,, | † | 8 20 | 8 0 | 9 30 | ... | 11 10 | 12 20 | 12 20 | ... | 1 30 | 2 20 | ... | 2 30 | 4 10 | ... | ... | 5 40 | ... | 7 0 | ... | ... | ... | ... | ... | ... |
| e ........arr. | 3 0 | 8 55 | 8 25 | 10 0 | 10 15 | 11 35 | 12 45 | 12 40 | 1 50 | 1 55 | 2 45 | 3 0 | 3 0 | 4 35 | 5 0 | 5 10 | 6 5 | 6 25 | 7 25 | ... | ... | ... | ... | ... | ... |
| es ...... ,, | ... | 9 15 | ... | ... | ... | .. | ... | 1 35 | ... | ... | ... | 3 35 | ... | 5 35 | ... | ... | ... | ... | ... |

## STEAM PACKET SERVICE FROM RYDE AND COWES—WEEK DAYS.

| | a.m. | a.m. | a.m. | a.m. | a.m. | a.m. | a.m. | p.m. | p.m. | p.m. | p.m. | p.m. | p.m. | p.m. | p.m. | p.m. | p.m. | p.m. |
|---|---|---|---|---|---|---|---|---|---|---|---|---|---|---|---|---|---|---|
| es...... dep. | ... | ... | ... | ... | 9 40 | ... | ... | ... | ... | 12 20 | ... | ... | 3 15 | ... | ... | 5 0 | ... | ... | ... | ... | ... |
| e ...... ,, | 7 15 | 8 0 | 9 0 | 10 10 | ... | 11 15 | 11 40 | 1 0 | 1 0 | 1 0 | 2 0 | 3 0 | 3 45 | 4 0 | 5 0 | 5 10 | 5 30 | 6 10 | 6 20 | 9 15 | ... | ... | ... |
| thsea arr. | ... | 8 25 | ... | 10 35 | ... | 11 40 | 12 5 | ... | 1 25 | 1 35 | ... | 3 25 | 4 20 | ... | ... | 5 35 | 6 5 | ... | 6 45 | * | ... | ... | ... |
| meouth (arbr. P.) ,, | 7 40 | 8 35 | 9 30 | 10 45 | 10 50 | 11 55 | ... | 1 30 | ... | 1 40 | 2 30 | 3 35 | 4 30 | 4 30 | 5 30 | ... | 6 15 | 6 40 | ... | ... | ... | ... |

## SUNDAYS.

| | a.m. | a.m. | a.m. | a.m. | p.m. | p.m. | p.m. | p.m. | | | a.m. | a.m. | a.m. | p.m. | p.m. | p.m. | p.m. |
|---|---|---|---|---|---|---|---|---|---|---|---|---|---|---|---|---|---|
| tsmth.(Har.Pr.)dep. | ... | 8 30 | 9 40 | 11 45 | 2 0 | 2 0 | ... | 6 10 | Cowes ............... dep. | ... | 10 0 | ... | ... | 4 0 | ... | ... |
| thsea ............... ,, | † | 8 40 | 10 0 | 12 0 | 2 15 | 2 10 | 4 0 | 6 30 | Ryde ..................... ,, | 7 40 | 10 30 | 11 0 | 1 0 | 2 50 | 4 25 | 5 0 | 9 15 |
| e................arr. | 3 0 | 9 10 | 10 30 | 12 25 | 2 40 | 2 50 | 4 30 | 6 55 | Southsea ............ arr. | 8 5 | 10 55 | 11 25 | 1 30 | 3 20 | 4 50 | 5 30 | * |
| es..................... ,, | ... | 9 45 | ... | ... | 3 15 | ... | ... | Portsmth.(Har.Pr.) ,, | 8 20 | 11 5 | 11 40 | 1 40 | ... | 5 0 | 5 40 | ... |

w Boat conveying Horses and Carriages to Portsmouth leaves Ryde at 10.0 a.m. and 3.0 p.m., and leaves Portsmouth for Ryde at 8.45 a.m. and 1.0 p.m.
small Steamer "Princess Louise" sails between East and West Cowes in connection with these Packets. Sundays excepted.
es Portsmouth Pier at 2.30 a.m.　* Runs to Portsmouth Pier only.

2. The first pier was built in 1814 and was gradually lengthened until a walk of nearly ½ mile became a passenger deterrent. The earlier method of disembarking into a horse-drawn cart (standing on the mud with its wheel hubs submerged in the sea) was less effort for the traveller but not ideal for crowds. A second pier was built adjacent to the first and a horse-operated tramway started operating on 27th August 1864. Note the crossover and siding.
(R. Brinton collection)

London Brighton & South Coast Railway.

Eridge to

# Ryde Pier

4. A rather faded view from about 1890 shows the new signal box and that the tramway no longer needed a crossover, since it only operated on the pier by that time. A small Manning Wardle steam locomotive was tried out prior to the opening of the line and a Merryweather was given trials in 1876. Two vertical-boilered engines were built by F. Bradley of Kidderminster and operated from 1881 until 1884 (when horses took over again). They were designed to be fired by town gas, held in a reservoir, but were in fact run on coke which was supplied by the gas works. (R. Brinton collection)

3. A much battered but interesting photograph from 1879 shows a third pier under construction, parallel to the previous two, which would permit railway trains to reach the Pier Head. Note the improved weather protection for waiting passengers. (R. Brinton collection)

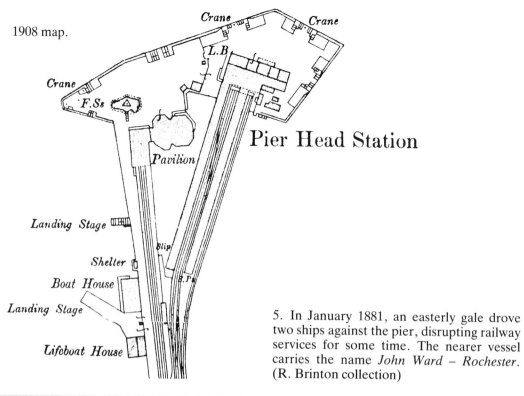

1908 map.

Crane     Crane

L.B

Crane

F.Ss

## Pier Head Station

Pavilion

Landing Stage

Slip

Shelter

S.P.

Boat House

Landing Stage

Lifeboat House

5. In January 1881, an easterly gale drove two ships against the pier, disrupting railway services for some time. The nearer vessel carries the name *John Ward – Rochester*. (R. Brinton collection)

6. A train from Cowes hauled by 2–4–0T *Shanklin* passes the last signal before the terminus. Notice how high the conductor rail is in relation to the tram running rails in the foreground. The pier was nearly blown up at the beginning of World War II by an obedient young army officer who had acted too literally upon instructions to destroy all south coast piers as a counter-measure to the invasion threat. (R. Silsbury collection)

7. The pier tramway was supplied with electric traction between 1886 and 1927, although the third rail appears to have deviated from its correct position in this view. The lack of decking meant that an inattentive tram conductor, when climbing from one car to the next, could quickly become like a herring – sliced up and pickled in brine. The screen from the prevailing wind and the scissors crossover are worth noting.
(R. Silsbury collection)

8. The Southern Railway came into being in January 1923 and five months later hired the Admiralty's floating crane from Portsmouth to transfer the first of the Adams class O2 tank locomotives from the mainland to the Pier Head. No. 211 is seen in the air, whilst no. 206 is still on the deck. *Sandown* is awaiting the return trip. Later the SR had its own floating crane at Southampton and transfers were made at Medina Wharf.
(D. Cullum collection)

10. TRAM CARS. PLEASE TENDER CORRECT FARE **2d**. The shelter had been improved but there could still be long queues and a long wait for a crowded and noisy apology for a tram. Many preferred to wait for a real train, your authors included.
(A. Blackburn)

**Joint Ryde Pier Railway.**
Available on the **DATE** of issue **ONLY**
This ticket is issued subject to the Regulations
& Conditions stated in the Joint Companies
Time Tables & Bills.

**RYDE [PIER HEAD]**
**to RYDE (St John's Rd.**
6d. SECOND CLASS. 6d.
Including 3d. for Ryde Pier Toll.

3301 3301 3301

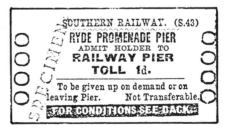

SOUTHERN RAILWAY. (S.43)
RYDE PROMENADE PIER
ADMIT HOLDER TO
**RAILWAY PIER**
**TOLL 1d.**
To be given up on demand or on
leaving Pier.    Not Transferable.
FOR CONDITIONS SEE BACK

SPECIMEN

0000 0000

←

9. In 1933, the SR carried out improvements which included an additional platform line (on the left). The platforms were renumbered 1 to 4 from east to west. The locomotives in this 1936 view are nos. 21 and 17, the latter with two discs indicating the Newport line. (S.W. Baker)

11. There were two Drewry built powered cars numbered 1 and 2, and two trailer cars, mysteriously numbered 7 and 8. The roof ventilators and opening windows were barely adequate in summer. (D.C. Callender/D. Cullum collection)

12. More internal combustion was to be found on the Pier Head in the form of Lister Auto Trucks which hauled parcels and an enormous traffic in "Passengers Luggage in Advance". No. T3 operated between 1934 and 1940. The gangplanks are little used since the installation of mechanically-operated ramps. (R. Silsbury collection)

13. The Westinghouse air pump on the smokebox and the air reservoir cylinder on the tank top are features to be seen in many of the following photographs. No. 18 *Ningwood* rumbles in on 29th March 1965, near the end of its journey and its life.
(J.A.M. Vaughan)

Bradshaw 1890

**RYDE, BEMBRIDGE, SANDOWN, and VENTNOR.—Isle of Wight and Ryde Pier.**
Trafl. Man., H. K. Day, Sandown, Isle of Wight.   Sec., R. Hicks, Sandown, Isle of Wight.

| Fares frm St. John's Rd | Down. | Week Days. | Sundays. |
|---|---|---|---|
| 1 cl. 2 cl. gov | | 1&2 1&2 1&2 1&2 1&2 1&2 1&2 1&2 1&2 1&2 1&2 1&2 1&2 | 1&2 1&2 1&2 1&2 1&2 1&2 1&2 |
| 1 0 0 10 | Ryde Pier Head ..dep | 8 0 9 16 10 22 12 51 10 2  8 3 15 4 12 5 25 6 38 7 4 29  0 | 9 25 1  0 .... 3  0 .... 7 35 8 36 |
| 0 60 5 | „ Esplanade | 8 4 9 20 10 26 12 9 1 14 2 11 3 19 4 15 5 19 6 42 7 4 39  5 | 9 29 1  5 .... 3  4 .... 7 39 8 40 |
| 1 cl. 2 cl. gov | „ St. John's Rd | 7 23 8 10 9 24 10 30 12 15 1 18 2 15 3 22 4 19 5 33 6 46 7 51 9 10 | 9 33 1 10 .... 3  8 .... 7 43 8 44 |
| 1 00 80 3½ | Brading Junction * | 7 36 8 19 9 32 10 39 12 23 1 26 2 23 3 30 4 27 5 41 6 54 8  0 9 19 | 9 41 1 18 .... 3 16 .... 7 51 8 52 |
| | Brading Junc...dep | * 32 .... 1051 ...... 1 38 .... 3 41 .... 5 52 .... 8 15 gov{ | 1 20 2 15 3 18 4 35 .... 9  5 |
| 1 5 1 0 0 5½ | St. Helen's | 8 37 .... 1056 .... 1 43 .... 3 46 .... 5 57 .... 8 40 Sats. only. { | 1 25 2 20 3 23 4 40 .... 9 10 |
| 1 7 1 10 6 | Bembridge ...arr | 8 43 .... 11 2 .... 1 49 .... 3 52 .... 6  3 .... 8 56 | 1 31 2 26 3 29 4 46 .... 9 16 |
| 1 6 1 0 0 5½ | Sandown Junc. † see | 7 42 8 25 9 38 1045 1228 1 32 2 29 3 35 4 33 5 46 7  0 8  9 23 | 9 47 1 24 .... 3 22 .... 7 56 8 57 |
| 2 0 1 4 0 7 | Shanklin ......[above] | 7 48 8 31 9 45 1051 1236 1 38 2 36 3 42 4 39 5 52 7  6 8 14 9 29 | 9 53 1 30 .... 3 28 .... 8 2 9 3 |
| 2 6 1 8 0 10 | Wroxall ‡ | 7 51 8 38 9 53 1058 1243 1 45 2 43 3 50 4 46 6  0 7 13 8 21 9 35 | 10 0 1 37 .... 3 34 .... 8 9 9 10 |
| 3 0 2 0 0 11½ | Ventnor § ...arr | 7 58 * 45 10 0 11 4 1249 1 51 2 51 3 56 4 52 6  7 20 8 27 9 40 | 10 5 1 43 .... 3 42 .... 8 14 9 15 |
| Fares. | Up. | 1&2 1&2 1&2 1&2 1&2 1&2 1&2 1&2 1&2 1&2 1&2 1&2 1&2 | 1&2 gov 1&2 1&2 1&2 1&2 |
| 1 cl. 2 cl. gov | Ventnor......dep | 7 28 8  5 9 20 1035 1210 1 12 2 10 3 15 4 15 5 25 6 42 7 50 8 40 9 45 | 1010 1 50 .... 4 10 8 40 .... |
| 0 60 40 1½ | Wroxall ‡ | ft 8 11 9 25 1031 1215 1 18 2 16 3 21 4 2 5 31 6 47 7 55 8 45 9 50 | 1016 1 56 .... 4 16 8 45 .... |
| 1 3 0 100 4 | Shanklin ...[above] | 7 38 8 18 9 32 1038 1222 1 25 2 23 3 28 4 27 5 39 6 54 8  2 8 51 9 57 | 1022 2  2 .... 4 22 8 51 .... |
| 1 6 1 20 6 | Sandown Jn.†(see | 7 42 8 25 9 38 1045 1228 1 32 2 29 3 35 4 33 5 46 7  0 8  8 57 10 2 | 1028 2  8 .... 4 28 8 57 .... |
| 2 6 1 10 010½ | Bembridge..dep | 8  7 .... 1027 .... 1 13 .... 3 19 .... 5 27 .... 7 48 Sats. only. { | 1  5 2  0 3  5 4 22 8 40 .... |
| 2 6 1 9 0 10 | St. Helen's | 8 12 .... 1032 .... 1 18 .... 3 23 .... 5 32 .... 7 53 Sats. only. { | 1 10 2  5 3 10 4 27 8 46 .... |
| | Brading Jnc. arr | 8 18 .... 1038 .... 1 24 .... 3 29 .... 5 38 .... 7 59 .... | 1 16 2 11 3 16 4 33 8 51 .... |
| 2 0 1 4 0 6 | Brading Jnc.* [70] | a 8 31 9 44 1050 1233 1 37 2 36 3 40 4 38 5 51 7 58 14 9  3 10 7 | 1034 2 14 .... 4 34 9  3 .... |
| 3 0 2 0 0 11½ | Ryde § 53,45,47 | .... 8 39 9 52 1057 1241 1 45 2 44 3 48 4 46 5 59 7 13 8 22 9 10 1015 | 1044 2 22 .... 4 44 9 10 .... |
| 3 6 2 51 3½ | „ Esplanade.. | 7 55 8 44 9 56 11 2 1245 1 50 2 48 3 52 4 50 6  3 7 17 8 26 9 14 .... | 1048 2 26 .... 4 48 9 14 .... |
| 4 0 2 10 1 4½ | „ Pier Head.. | a 7 58 8 48 10 0 11 5 1249 1 54 2 52 3 56 4 53 6  6 7 20 8 30 9 18 .... | 1052 2 30 .... 4 52 9 18 .... |

* Station for Yaverland and the Roman Villa ; † for Lake, Carisbrooke Castle, and Parkhurst ; ‡ for Appuldercombe and Godshill; § for Bonchurch, The Landslip, St. Lawrence, Niton, Blackgang, Freshwater, and Alum Bay.

‖ St. John's Road.   a Stops by signal to take up for Portsmouth, London, and Brighton.

14. A Grafton steam crane was used in the dismantling operation prior to electrification of train services. Railway life at this spot had its benefits – staff were reputed never to be short of fish in their larders and firemen were known to cool off with a swim between trips! Conversely, the station was a target for a German airman's machine gun. The booking clerk saved his life by putting his head in the safe. (G. Holmes)

0000

**SOUTHERN RAILWAY.**
CIRCULAR TOUR (No.1)
Available as advertised.
Sandown or Shanklin to
**(F.G.) RYDE**
Via Brading
by Rail
Including Pier Tolls
Exclusive of Tramway or Train
THIRD CLASS
**FOR CONDITIONS
SEE BACK.**
**SOUTHERN RAILWAY.**
CIRCULAR TOUR (No.1)
Available as advertised.
(G) Ryde Pier to
SANDOWN PIER or
SHANKLIN PIER
direct by S. R. Coy's Steamer
Including Pier Tolls
Exclusive of Tramway or Train

0000

**JOINT RAILWAY STEAMER.**
Available on the DATE of issue ONLY.
This ticket is issued subject to the Regulations
& Conditions stated in the Joint Companies
Time Tables & Bills.
9566
BOAT No. 1
**RYDE TO
PORTSMOUTH**
EXCESS FARE TO 4d.
FIRST
To be given on landing.
9566

15. By 1975 the scissors crossover at the approach to the station was worn out and a replacement was manufactured at Redbridge. It was never installed, due to cranage problems and reduced traffic, eventually being sold to the Bluebell Railway. The crossing and signal box was removed, the Pier line becoming two single tracks, the eastward one carrying a shuttle service to the Esplanade at peak traffic times only. (J. Scrace)

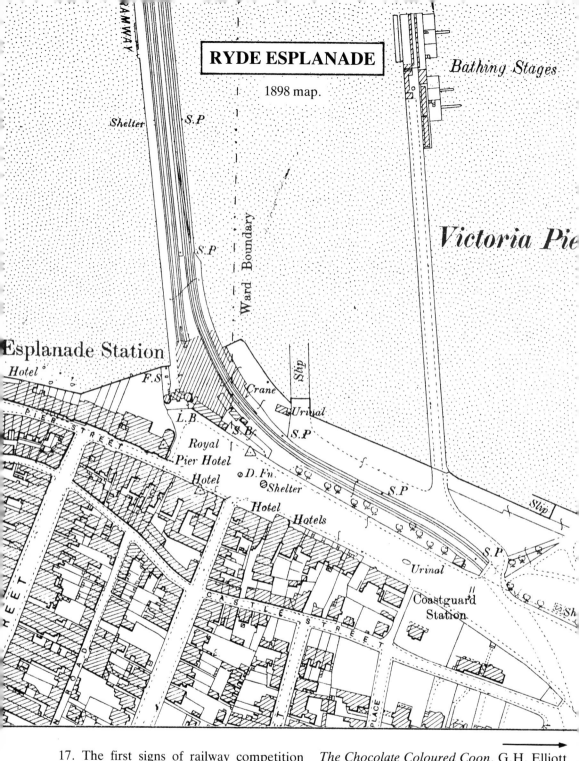

**RYDE ESPLANADE**

1898 map.

*Bathing Stages*

*Victoria Pie*

Shelter  S.P.

Ward Boundary

S.P.

Esplanade Station

Hotel

F.S.

Crane

Ship

Urinal

L.B.

S.B.

S.P.

Royal
Pier Hotel

Hotel

D. Fn.

Shelter

Hotel  Hotels

S.P

Slip

S.P.

Urinal

Coastguard
Station

PIER STREET

CASTLE STREET

PLACE

Sh

17. The first signs of railway competition appeared in 1905 when four open-top buses arrived on the Island. They were not successful and in 1907 a railway official glibly remarked that buses presented no threat. *The Chocolate Coloured Coon*, G.H. Elliott and his company appear in this photograph, celebrating the commencement of a Milnes-Daimler operated service. (G. Holmes collection)

16. There are many details worthy of study here. The road transport; the architecture; the boats at anchor and the profusion of pier pedestrians. (Lens of Sutton)

18. The Joint Railway Committee tug *Ada* appears to have crossed the Spithead with two tow boats loaded with horses, probably bound for Ashey races. The boats would then be poled onto the slipway; the rudder removed and the stern opened. All cattle and motor vehicles crossed in this manner until 1927, when end loading vessels started to operate to Fishbourne. In 1912, tow boats left Portsmouth Point at 8.45 am and 1 pm; Ryde departures were at 10 am and 3 pm. Drovers crossed free of charge – only if accompanying animals. *Ada* was driven against the pier by an easterly gale in about 1914 and destroyed. At low tide motor vehicles disembarking into shallow water were frequently left stuck in the mud and so the service became tidal. The area is now part of the Hover Terminal. Progress indeed! (R. Silsbury collection)

London Brighton & South Coast Railway.

Ryde Esplanade to

# Eastbourne

"Good Lines" – The Monthly Journal of the
Commercial Travellers Christian Association

19. Steam railcars became popular in the Edwardian era and on 4th October 1906, the IOWCR's new purchase was delivered to St. Helens Quay. The carriage part was built by Hurst Nelson & Co and seated six 1st class and 44 2nd class passengers. The engine portion at the far end was from R. & W. Hawthorn & Co., and was supplied by a boiler 4'6" long and 3'6" diameter. It was moderately successful but the Siamese twins were finally separated in 1910 and rebuilt.
(R. Silsbury collection)

The Pier, Ryde, I.W.

20. Points of interest in this view are the road transport; the wharf (complete with bollards and crane) and part of the former signal box (closed in 1923) which has been incorporated into the lean-to by the foot crossing. The tramway route was between the railings in the foreground, before the arrival of the railway. (R. Silsbury collection)

21. Bus competition began to make inroads into local railway traffic in particular, in the 1920s. However, tourism was developing and so did the railways of the Island. This 26-seater Daimler, photographed on 2nd October 1925, was typical of the period, so were the solid rear and pneumatic front tyres. (L.L. Cooper/A.A.F. Bell collection)

22. When no. 6 was purchased in 1890, the IWC passengers were still being treated to goods train standard of braking. It was to be another four years before continuous brakes were fitted to all their coaches and locomotives. This engine was the first one bought ready equipped and was built by Black, Hawthorn & Co. The wharf crane is in the background and the coach is an ex-IWR four-wheeler. (J.G. Sturt)

**Ryde.**—Often very cold in the streets that straighten to the sea, but the houses are so good and the sanitation and water supply so excellent that Ryde would always have a great sanitary following.

1928 Guide Book.

23. Ex-IWCR 2–4–0T no. 8 rounds the 9 chain curve, just above the high tide mark. The SR inherited an odd mixture of vintage rolling stock in 1923. This little Beyer Peacock machine lasted until 1929. (R.B. Owen collection)

24. Another Pier Head bound train, this time climbing the 1 in 50 gradient between the tunnel and the station. The Joint Committee chose to pass their new line under the highway in view of the local aggravation that the tramway level crossing had caused. They did not foresee that by restricting the height to almost 12'3" (mainland loading gauge is 13'1") they would cause aggravation to successive railway managers. (R. Silsbury collection)

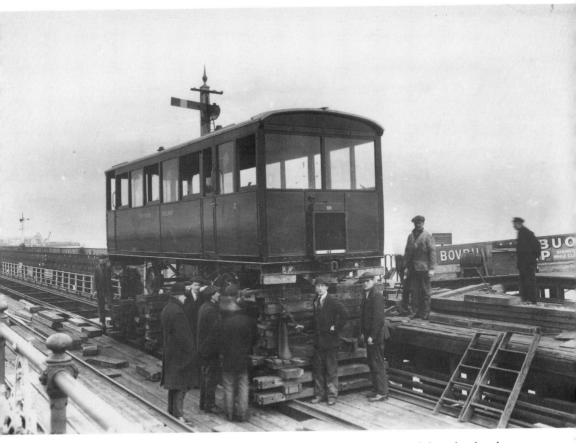

25. The current for the electric tramway had been generated since 1885 by a Siemens dynamo turned by an Otto gas engine. By 1927 this equipment was exhausted and the SR decided to provide two petrol-driven vehicles but to retain the trailer cars. Here we see Drewry car no.2 arriving, having been jacked across the platform from the main line. They were built with Bagulay engines which were replaced with 26HP Bedfords after World War II and diesels in 1959-60. (Lens of Sutton)

SOUTHERN RAILWAY.

(9/23)                                        787

TO

RYDE ESPLANADE

26. The electric motor car is seen here departing and in the foreground is the *Grapes Car*. It was built at Ryde in about 1867 as a 1st class, with seats on the roof and ran until damaged in 1935. This teak and mahogany gem is preserved in Hull Museum. Trailer no. 7 arrived in 1936 and no. 8 in the following year. As the new electric trains offered improvements in all respects, the tramway closed in January 1969. (Lens of Sutton)

SOUTHERN RAILWAY.
Issued subject to the directors, Regulations &
Conditions of the Company's Bills and Notices.

H.M.F. on LEAVE.

Ryde Esplanade to

Ryde Esplanade
Newport

Ryde Esplanade
Newport

NEWPORT

Via Ausry.

THIRD CLASS
NOT TRANSFERABLE.

THIRD CLASS

SOUTHERN RAILWAY.

RYDE PROMENADE PIER.

**DECK CHAIR** 3d.

This ticket to be retained and shewn on demand.          Not Transferable.

The Company shall not be liable for personal injury( whether fatal or otherwise ), loss, damage, delay or detention of or to the holder and/or his/her property by whomsoever caused and whether occasioned by neglect or otherwise.

| Morning | Afternoon | Evening |
|---------|-----------|---------|
| 9 - 1   | 1 - 5     | 5 - Dusk |

27. The gradient between the tunnel and the station is quite apparent in this July 1935 view of no. 21 *Sandown*. Beach huts stood peacefully where hovercraft now roar. (S.W. Baker)

28. During the period that the horse-drawn tramway ran between the Esplanade and St. John's Road, it passed through an archway on the ground floor of this house which is situated on the corner of The Strand and Cornwall Street. The large bay window was added when the archway was filled in. (V. Mitchell)

30. No.28 *Ashey* accelerates down to the tunnel on 23rd July 1966, the last summer of steam. The tunnel is below high tide level and is therefore prone to flooding. The structure on the left houses the pumps to keep it clear of water. Originally they were operated by Crossley engines working on town gas but in 1909 electric motors were fitted and subsequently a Lister standby petrol engine has also been installed. (S.C. Nash)

29. During the winter of 1963-64 the superstructure of the railway pier was partly renewed necessitating suspension of train services and transfers of passengers to the trams. The following winter, Cowes trains terminated at St. John's Road requiring a change to another steam train there and then to a tram at Esplanade. (J.A.M. Vaughan)

31. The engine of this south-bound train is almost level with milepost 1 whilst the rear vehicle is level with the gate of the private siding to the gasworks. The wagon in the lower left is standing on a turntable from which a short siding ran westwards. Loaded coal wagons were brought from Medina Wharf and locomotives were permitted to propel up to 15 wagons back to St. John's Road on the up line as no crossover was provided. The siding closed in about 1955. (R.B. Owen collection)

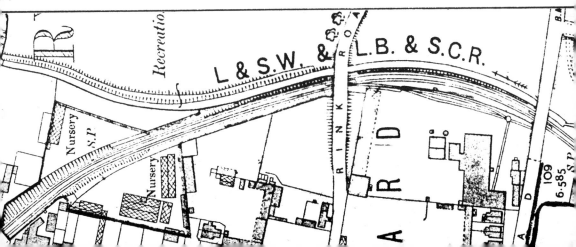

## Return Tickets at Single Fares by all Trains on Sundays.

## ISLE OF WIGHT RAILWAY.

### Local Service between Ryde and Ventnor, with Steam Packet Connections.

| | STATIONS. | DOWN TRAINS—Week Days. | | | | | | | | | | | | | | Sundays. | | | |
|---|---|---|---|---|---|---|---|---|---|---|---|---|---|---|---|---|---|---|---|
| | | 1 2 & P. | 1 & 2 | 1 & 2 | 1 & 2 | 1 & 2 | 1 & 2 | 1 & 2 | 1 & 2 | 1 & 2 | 1 & 2 | 1 & 2 | 1 & 2 | | | 1 2 & P. | 1 & 2 | 1 & 2 | 1 & 2 |
| | | a.m. | a.m. | a.m. | a.m. | a.m. | p.m. | a.m. | p.m. | p.m. | p.m. | p.m. | p.m. | p.m. | | | a.m. | a.m. | p.m. | p.m. |
| Steam Packets. | Lymington to Ryde by boat dep. | ... | ... | ... | ... | ... | ... | ... | ... | ... | ... | ... | ... | | ... | ... | ... | ... | ... | ... |
| | Yarmouth „ ...... „ | ... | ... | ... | ... | ... | ... | ... | ... | ... | ... | ... | ... | | ... | ... | ... | ... | ... | ... |
| | Southampton „ | ... | ... | ... | 8 30 | ... | ... | 11 10 | ... | 2 0 | ... | 3 55 | ... | | | ... | ... | 8 45 | ... | 2 30 |
| | Cowes to Ryde ...... „ | ... | ... | ... | 9 40 | ... | ... | 12 20 | ... | 3 15 | ... | 5 15 | ... | | | ... | ... | 10 0 | ... | 4 0 |
| | Portsmouth (Victoria Pier) „ | ... | ... | 8 10 | 9 45 | ... | 11 45 | ... | 1 45 | 2 45 | 4 10 | ... | 5 45 | | Saturdays only. | ... | 8 35 | 11 55 | 1 55 | 5 5 |
| | Southsea Pier ............ „ | ... | ... | 8 20 | 10 0 | ... | 12 0 | ... | 2 0 | 3 0 | 4 20 | ... | 6 0 | | | ... | 8 40 | 12 0 | 2 0 | 6 0 |
| | Stokes Bay „ ...... „ | ... | ... | ... | ... | 10 40 | 11 50 | ... | 2 15 | ... | 4 40 | ... | 6 30 | | | ... | ... | ... | ... | ... |
| | Portsmouth Harbour Stn.. „ | ... | ... | 8 0 | 9 50 | ... | 12 10 | 1 10 | 2 40 | ... | 4 30 | 5 20 | 6 40 | | | ... | 8 30 | 11 50 | 1 50 | 5 45 |
| R. P. Ry. | Ryde (Pier Head)............dep. | **A** | ... | 9 10 | 10 40 | 11 50 | 1 7 | 2 0 | 3 15 | 4 5 | 5 15 | 6 15 | 7 25 | ... | | ... | 9 20 | 12 45 | 2 35 | 6 45 |
| | Ryde (Pier Gates) ...... „ | | ... | 9 13 | 10 43 | 11 53 | 1 10 | 2 3 | 3 18 | 4 8 | 5 18 | 6 18 | 7 28 | ... | | ... | 9 23 | 12 48 | 2 38 | 6 48 |
| | Ryde (St. John's Road) ...... arr. | | ... | 9 20 | 10 50 | 12 0 | 1 17 | 2 10 | 3 25 | 4 15 | 5 25 | 6 25 | 7 35 | ... | | ... | 9 30 | 12 55 | 2 45 | 6 55 |
| I. of Wight Ry. | RYDE (St. John's Road) ...dep. | 7 25 | 8 15 | 9 25 | 10 55 | 12 5 | 1 22 | 2 15 | 3 28 | 4 20 | 5 30 | 6 30 | 7 59 | 9 0 | | ... | 9 30 | 12 55 | 2 50 | 7 1 |
| | Brading (1) ...................... „ | 7 33 | 8 23 | 9 33 | 11 4 | 12 13 | 1 31 | 2 23 | 3 36 | 4 28 | 5 38 | 6 39 | 7 58 | 9 9 | | ... | 9 38 | 1 3 | 2 59 | 7 2 |
| | Sandown (2) ...... „ | 7 39 | 8 28 | 9 39 | 11 9 | 12 20 | 1 38 | 2 29 | 3 44 | 4 34 | 5 44 | 6 46 | 8 4 | 9 15 | | ... | 9 44 | 1 9 | 3 6 | 7 3 |
| | Shanklin ...... „ | 7 45 | 8 34 | 9 46 | 11 15 | 12 27 | 1 44 | 2 36 | 3 51 | 4 40 | 5 50 | 6 53 | 8 10 | 9 21 | | ... | 9 50 | 1 15 | 3 13 | 7 3 |
| | Wroxall (3) ...... „ | 7 53 | 8 42 | 9 55 | 11 23 | 12 36 | 1 52 | 2 45 | 4 0 | 4 48 | 5 58 | 7 2 | 8 18 | 9 29 | | ... | 9 58 | 1 23 | 3 22 | 7 4 |
| | VENTNOR (4) ............ arr. | 8 0 | 8 48 | 10 2 | 11 29 | 12 42 | 1 58 | 2 52 | 4 7 | 4 54 | 6 4 | 7 9 | 8 24 | 9 35 | | ... | 10 4 | 1 29 | 3 29 | 7 5 |

**A.**—Third Class Return Tickets, issued by these Train, are available only to return by the 1.0 and 6.25 p.m. Up Trains.

(1) Station for Yaverland and Bembridge. (2) For Lake, Newport Junction Line, Carisbrook Castle and Parkhurst. (3) For Appuldurcombe S and Godshill. (4) For Bonchurch, and "The Landslip," The Undercliff, St. Lawrence, Niton, Blackgang, Freshwater and Alum Bay.

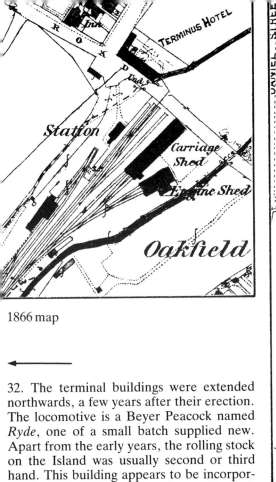

1866 map

32. The terminal buildings were extended northwards, a few years after their erection. The locomotive is a Beyer Peacock named *Ryde*, one of a small batch supplied new. Apart from the early years, the rolling stock on the Island was usually second or third hand. This building appears to be incorporated in the present structure. (Lens of Sutton)

Points of particular interest in the 1878 timetable are the separate times for the Ryde Pier Railway's trams and the wild claim in note 2.

I. of W. Steam Packet Co. Ltd.
This Ticket is issued subject to the Bye-laws Regulations & Conditions stated in the Companies' Time Tables, Bills & Notices Available on DAY of issue ONLY.

**COWES WEST PIER** to
Cowes W. Pier                Cowes W. Pier
Ryde St. J. Rd               Ryde St. J. Rd

**RYDE ST. JOHN'S RD**
INCLUDING PIER TOLLS
Via Direct Boat & Tram

Third Class                  Third Class
Fare 1/5                     Fare 1/5

0012    0012

1908 map.

33. The covered footbridge obscures the road bridge with which it was directly linked for many years. This 1920 view shows the mid-platform crossover and part of the locomotive and carriage works. SR rationalisation in 1925 concentrated locomotive maintenance here and carriage work at Newport.
(P. Rutherford/D. Cullum collection)

34. A northbound train passes the 1874 locomotive shed, sometime after the grouping in 1923. The shed was situated some distance to the south of the station (see 1908 map) and was proving inadequate for the expanding traffic. A new shed was opened in May 1930, which could house eight engines.
(R. Silsbury collection)

# Isle of Wight Railway

## TO

# RYDE

## St. John's Road.

35. Beyond the train is the South Box and the goods shed. Both were soon replaced under the SR improvement scheme. No. 14 *Shanklin* was one of the new Beyer Peacocks supplied to the IWR and was scrapped in 1927. (R. Silsbury collection)

36. A transitional view showing the larger 1926 signal box and gantry but with the early dilapidated goods shed beyond. The Island usually escapes severe snow storms but, on Boxing Day 1962, the 8.15 am mail train took 11¼ hours to reach Ventnor. This was the beginning of the worst winter in living memory, when even the sea froze.
(R. Silsbury collection)

37. The new locomotive shed was built, close to the station approach. The new partly roofed coaling stage can also be seen. Locomotive cleaning standards were very high in those days of low labour costs. Note the burnished buffers on no. 20 *Shanklin*.
(J.A.G. Coltas)

38. By 1933 the asbestos cladding had become a little smoke stained but even a humble Terrier would come "off shed" immaculate. No. 13 *Carisbrooke* had been formerly LBSCR no. 77 *Wonersh* and was on the Island from 1927 to 1949. The PLA van was to be used exclusively for "Passengers Luggage in Advance" to prevent complaints about holiday clothes smelling of stale fish, the traditional odour of mixed traffic vans in the days of wet fish travelling to fishmongers in leaking boxes. (J.A.G. Coltas)

Bradshaw 1910

| Up. | | | | | Week Days. | | | | | | | | | | | | | Sundays. | | | | |
|---|---|---|---|---|---|---|---|---|---|---|---|---|---|---|---|---|---|---|---|---|---|---|
| | | 1&2 | | 1&2 | 1&2 | mrn | mrn | 1&2 | 1&2 | 1&2 | aft | 1&2 | 1&2 | 1&2 | aft | 1&2 | aft | aft | aft | mrn | 1&2 | 1&2 | 1&2 | aft |
| Ventnor ..................dep | 6 30 | | 7 25 | | 8 8 | 9 20 | 10 20 | 12 8 | 1 8 | 2 8 | 3 23 | 4 15 | 4 40 | 5 33 | 6 40 | 8 5 | 8 25 | 9 55 | 1015 | | 1 55 | | 4 12 | 8 35 |
| 1¼ Wroxall §§ .................. | a | | a | | 8 13 | 9 25 | 10 25 | 12 13 | 1 13 | 2 13 | 3 28 | 4 20 | 4 45 | 5 38 | 6 45 | 8 10 | | 8 40 | 10 0 | 1020 | 2 0 | | 4 17 | 8 40 |
| 4¼ Shanklin.................... | 6 40 | | 7 35 | | 8 21 | 9 32 | 10 33 | 12 20 | 1 21 | 2 19 | 3 35 | 4 28 | 4 51 | 5 45 | 6 52 | 8 16 | | 8 47 | 10 6 | 1026 | 2 6 | | 4 24 | 8 47 |
| 6¼ Sandown Junction 172 ........ | 6 45 | | 7 40 | | 8 27 | 9 38 | 1040 | 1227 | 1 28 | 2 25 | 3 41 | 4 34 | 4 57 | 5 50 | 6 58 | 8 22 | | 8 53 | 1011 | 1031 | 2 11 | | 4 30 | 8 53 |
| Mls Bembridge.............dep | 6 55 | | 7 30 | | 8 9 | 9 18 | 1030 | 1218 | 1 18 | 2 7 | 3 30 | 4 28 | ... | 5 30 | ... | 8 15 | 8 45 | ... | ... | ... | 1 10 | 2 53 | 10 4 | 2 08 | 8 30 |
| 1¼ St. Helens ........ | 6 40 | | 7 35 | | 8 13 | 9 24 | 1035 | 1223 | 1 23 | 2 12 | 3 35 | 4 33 | ... | 5 36 | 6 55 | 8 20 | 8 50 | ... | ... | ... | 1 15 | 2 10 | 3 15 | 4 25 | 8 35 |
| 2½ Brading Junction ‡ .......arr | 6 45 | | 7 40 | | 8 18 | 9 29 | 1040 | 1228 | 1 28 | 2 17 | 3 40 | 4 38 | ... | 5 41 | 7 08 | 8 25 | 8 55 | ... | ... | ... | 1 20 | 2 15 | 3 20 | 4 30 | 8 40 |
| 7¾ Brading Junction ‡ .......... | a | | a | | 8 32 | 9 44 | 1046 | 1232 | 1 34 | 2 30 | 3 46 | 4 40 | 5 2 | 5 57 | 7 5 | 8 28 | | 8 59 | 1016 | 1036 | 2 16 | | 4 36 | 8 59 |
| 1½ Ryde (St. John's Road) ...... | a | | a | | 8 40 | 9 52 | 1053 | 1240 | 1 42 | 2 38 | 3 54 | 4 48 | 5 10 | 6 2 | 7 13 | 8 36 | | 9 7 | 1024 | 1044 | 2 24 | | 4 43 | 9 7 |
| 2¼ " (Esplanade) .....|187 | | | 7 0 | | 8 44 | 9 56 | 1057 | 1244 | 1 47 | 2 42 | 3 58 | 4 52 | 5 14 | 6 6 | 7 17 | 8 40 | | 9 12 | ... | 1048 | 2 28 | | 4 47 | 9 12 |
| 2¾ " (Pier Head)131,139,142 ar | 7 0 | | 7 55 | | 8 48 | 10 0 | 11 2 | 1248 | 1 50 | 2 45 | 4 2 | 4 56 | 5 18 | 6 10 | 7 20 | 8 44 | | 9 16 | ... | 1052 | 2 32 | | 4 51 | 9 16 |
| 6¼ 131 WATERLOO (via Stokes Bay) arr | | | 7 55 | | 1139 | ... | ... | 1 2 | 4 48 | 7 31 | ... | 8 3 | ... | 9 6 | ... | ... | ... | ... | ... | ... | ... | 10 33 | 3 35 | ... |
| 1¼ 131 " (via Portsmouth)139 " | 9 55 | | 1133 | | ... | 1 45 | ... | 4 33 | ... | ... | 7 37 | ... | 10 5 | ... | ... | ... | ... | ... | ... | ... | ... | 8 10 | ... | ... |
| 3¾ 187 LONDON BRIDGE " | | | 1042 | | ... | 1 52 | ... | 4 25 | 10 ... | 7 41 | ... | ... | 10 3 | ... | ... | ... | ... | ... | ... | ... | ... | 8 5 | ... | ... |
| 3¾ 187 VICTORIA " | | | 1050 | | | | | | | | | | | | | | | | | | | | | |

a Stop by Signal to take up for Portsmouth, London, and Brighton.   s Saturdays only.
‡‡ Station for Yaverland (1¼ miles), the Roman Villa (1 mile), and Nunwell (1¼ miles);   §§ for Appuldurcombe (¾ mile).

39. The "secondhand" tradition mentioned earlier applied even to engine sheds. Whilst the cladding was new, the steel spans and supports had previously been part of the LBSCR's overhead electrification equipment in South London. Cleaning standards dropped towards the end of steam. Poor *Seaview* and *Brading* had seen better days. (E. Wilmshurst)

40. Even the signal box was secondhand. It had previously been located at Waterloo Junction, now Waterloo East. The 45-lever frame today controls all operations between Pier Head and Smallbrook Junction. The extent of the coaling stage shelter and the ash heaps can be more clearly seen in this 1961 view. (R.S. Greenwood)

41. A fine view on a fine evening in July 1961 of no. 20 *Shanklin* bringing in a six coach train from Ventnor. The massive coal bunker is obvious in this view. Enlarged bunkers were fitted in the early 1930s so that engines could remain in traffic for longer periods, a valuable feature particularly on peak summer Saturdays. (R.S. Greenwood)

42. Cowes trains were limited to five coaches, the headcode being a "white" disc above each buffer. The van on the right was created about 1956 from a former SECR coach. Compare the workshop roof with earlier views. Photograph date – 23rd July 1961. (R.S. Greenwood)

# ISLE OF WIGHT RAILWAY AND COACH SERVICES

## RYDE to VENTNOR.

| | WEEK DAYS | | | | | | | | | | | | | SUNDAYS | | | |
|---|---|---|---|---|---|---|---|---|---|---|---|---|---|---|---|---|---|
| | 1 2 P | 1 & 2 | 1 & 2 | 1 & 2 | 1 & 2 | 1 & 2 | 1 & 2 | 1 & 2 | 1 & 2 | 1 & 2 | 1 & 2 | 1 & 2 | 1 & 2 C | 1 & 3 | 1 & 2 | 1 & 2 | 1 & 2 |
| | a.m. | a.m. | a.m. | a.m. | p.m. | p.m. | p.m. | p.m. | p.m. | p.m. | p.m. | p.m. | p.m. | a.m. | p.m. | p.m. | p.m. |
| RYDE PIER HEAD ......dep. | ... | 8 6 | 9 16 | 10 33 | 12 10 | 1 10 | 2 21 | 3 19 | 4 8 | 5 31 | 6 37 | 7 45 | 8 55 | 9 25 | 12 45 | 2 50 | 7 35 |
| Ryde (Esplanade).......... ,, | ... | 8 10 | 9 20 | 10 37 | 12 14 | 1 14 | 2 24 | 3 23 | 4 12 | 5 35 | 6 41 | 7 49 | 9 0 | 9 29 | 12 49 | 2 55 | 7 39 |
| Ryde (St. John's Road) ...... ,, | 7 25 | 8 14 | 9 24 | 10 41 | 12 18 | 1 18 | 2 28 | 3 27 | 4 16 | 5 39 | 6 45 | 7 53 | 9 5 | 9 33 | 12 53 | 3 0 | 7 43 |
| Brading ........ ,, | 7 33 | 8 22 | 9 32 | 10 49 | 12 26 | 1 26 | 2 36 | 3 35 | 4 24 | 5 48 | 6 53 | 8 1 | 9 13 | 9 41 | 1 3 | 3 8 | 7 51 |
| Sandown ........ ,, | 7 39 | 8 28 | 9 38 | 10 55 | 12 32 | 1 32 | 2 42 | 3 41 | 4 30 | 5 53 | 6 59 | 8 7 | 9 20 | 9 47 | 1 7 | 3 14 | 7 57 |
| Shanklin ........ ,, | 7 45 | 8 34 | 9 44 | 11 1 | 12 38 | 1 38 | 2 48 | 3 47 | 4 37 | 5 59 | 7 5 | 8 13 | 9 26 | 9 53 | 1 13 | 3 20 | 8 3 |
| Wroxall ........ ,, | 7 52 | 8 41 | 9 51 | 11 8 | 12 45 | 1 45 | 2 55 | 3 54 | 4 44 | 6 6 | 7 12 | 8 20 | 9 33 | 10 0 | 1 20 | 3 28 | 8 10 |
| VENTNOR ........arr. | 7 58 | 8 48 | 9 58 | 11 15 | 12 52 | 1 51 | 3 1 | 4 0 | 4 50 | 6 12 | 7 19 | 8 27 | 9 40 | 10 5 | 1 27 | 3 34 | 8 17 |

## VENTNOR to RYDE.

| | 1 2 P | 1 & 2 | 1 & 2 | 1 & 2 | 1 & 2 | 1 & 2 | 1 & 2 | 1 & 2 | 1 & 2 | 1 & 2 | 1 & 2 | 1 & 2 | 1 2 P | 1 & 2 | 1 & 2 | 1 & 2 |
|---|---|---|---|---|---|---|---|---|---|---|---|---|---|---|---|---|
| | a.m. | a.m. | a.m. | p.m. | p.m. | p.m. | p.m. | p.m. | p.m. | p.m. | p.m. | | a.m. | p.m. | p.m. | p.m. |
| VENTNOR ......dep. | 8 8 | 9 20 | 10 23 | 12 0 | 1 12 | 2 10 | 3 10 | 4 10 | 5 22 | 6 41 | 7 47 | 8 35 | 10 10 | 1 45 | 4 10 | 8 30 |
| Wroxall ........ ,, | 8 14 | 9 25 | 10 29 | 12 6 | 1 18 | 2 16 | 3 16 | 4 16 | 5 28 | 6 46 | 7 53 | 8 40 | 10 16 | 1 51 | 4 16 | 8 35 |
| Shanklin ........ ,, | 8 21 | 9 32 | 10 36 | 12 13 | 1 25 | 2 23 | 3 23 | 4 23 | 5 35 | 6 53 | 8 0 | 8 46 | 10 22 | 1 57 | 4 22 | 8 42 |
| Sandown ........ ,, | 8 28 | 9 38 | 10 43 | 12 20 | 1 32 | 2 29 | 3 30 | 4 30 | 5 42 | 6 59 | 8 7 | 8 51 | 10 28 | 2 3 | 4 28 | 8 48 |
| Brading ........ ,, | 8 34 | 9 44 | 10 49 | 12 26 | 1 38 | 2 36 | 3 35 | 4 36 | 5 48 | 7 5 | 8 13 | 8 56 | 10 34 | 2 9 | 4 34 | 8 54 |
| Ryde (St. John's Road) ...... ,, | 8 42 | 9 52 | 10 57 | 12 34 | 1 46 | 2 44 | 3 43 | 4 44 | 5 55 | 7 13 | 8 21 | 9 5 | 10 44 | 2 17 | 4 44 | 9 2 |
| Ryde (Esplanade).......... ,, | 8 46 | 9 56 | 11 1 | 12 38 | 1 50 | 2 48 | 3 47 | 4 48 | 6 0 | 7 17 | 8 25 | 9 9 | 10 48 | 2 21 | 4 48 | 9 6 |
| RYDE PIER HEAD ......arr. | 8 50 | 10 0 | 11 5 | 12 42 | 1 54 | 2 52 | 3 51 | 4 51 | 6 4 | 7 21 | 8 29 | 9 13 | 10 52 | 2 25 | 4 52 | 9 10 |

C   Saturdays only.

43. No. 33 *Bembridge* struggles to keep her feet with an unusually long freight train, in June 1963. In fact it is two trains – an engineer's train plus empty coal wagons – hence the three brake vans. The line southwards was operated as two single tracks in winter and double track in the summer. Two of the four signal arms were removed during the latter period. (D. Fereday Glenn)

44. At the south end of the station on 21st December 1966, we see a Shanklin train arriving, preceded by its own smoke. The locomotive and wagon are stabled on the up line, which was out of use due to engineering work – note the conductor rail insulators. The co-acting semaphores and the banner repeater signal on the right were about to become obsolete. (J.A.M. Vaughan)

45. The signal box now controls a few semaphore signals within the station confines, the
more remote ones being colour light. The
former loop line next to the shed is now a
carriage cleaning siding and the works under-
takes all maintenance and painting of the
electric stock. The box looks very smart in
this 1974 view. (J. Scrace)

46. This 1985 view shows double capitals on
the stanchions with fine tracery and the IWR
monogram cast into the spandrel brackets.
These features can be enjoyed today despite
the roof having been shortened, as shown. A
shortage of seats prompted the use of the
platform edge as an alternative. (V. Mitchell)

47. The works has now had a tradition of over 120 years of ingenuity and enterprise in maintaining largely obsolete rolling stock with limited equipment, itself often being obsolete. The locomotive is ex-IWCR No. 4, another Beyer Peacock to arrive new on the Island. It was built in 1876 and scrapped in 1925. (R.B. Owen collection)

49. Known locally as the *Porcupine*, this ex-LCDR coach was fitted with hinged projections for testing clearances. This 1932 photograph shows a remarkable profusion of spines at platform level.
(A.B. MacLeod/Wight Loco. Soc.)

48. To avoid steaming a locomotive specially for works shunting, this unique machine was designed and built in the works in 1929. It had 14" driving wheels, a 5 ft wheelbase and was capable of moving 20 tons, given a muscular crew. It survived until 1938. (H.C. Casserley)

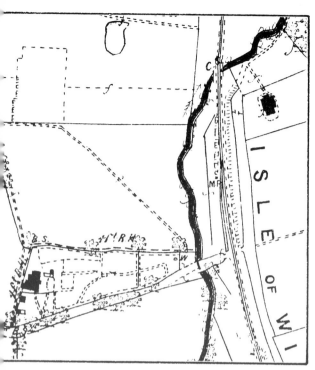

The 1866 map shows that before the additional line was laid down for the IWCR, a short siding was provided for agricultural traffic presumably, almost ¼ mile north of Smallbrook Lane brige.

50. Ten days before the end of steam no. 27 *Merstone* runs southwards on the up road. When this track had been used as two single lines, it had often been the scene of unofficial races between loco crews. Similar races took place on leaving another island junction of similar name – St. Johns, Isle of Man. (J.A.M. Vaughan)

WHISTLE

# SMALLBROOK JUNCTION

51. The 15.32 from Ventnor passes by the rusty junction on 16th May 1964, with the line to Cowes on the right. As at St. John's Road, the semaphore arms were removed during the winter. By 1935, it was claimed to be the busiest single line junction in the country with 12 trains per hour and was manned from 3.45 am to 11.30 pm. It had a 20-lever knee frame. (S.C. Nash)

52. The privy in the bushes; the fresh water can and the oil lamp standards all confirm that there were no main services at this remote location. The signal box had been opened on 18th July 1926, minus a roof due to strike delays. The signal was built by the SR using two lengths of secondhand rail. Note the treadle in the foreground which prevented the facing points being inadvertently moved under a passing train. (J. Scrace)

# BRADING

53. When the railway arrived at Brading in 1864, it was still a fishing village with a quay on the navigable River Yar. A siding was laid down to the quay. Jabez Balfour was authorised to construct a sea wall between St. Helens and Bembridge and also to reclaim the land within the Yar estuary. His financial problems necessitated him taking refuge in Argentina but he eventually returned to the Island where he became a long-term resident – in Parkhurst Prison. The top-hatted station master is standing by a LSWR poster announcing quick trains from Stokes Bay to London. (Lens of Sutton)

→

54. A splendid post card view from about 1910 shows the Bembridge branch bay platform on the left occupied by *Shanklin* with two spare coaches in the siding. *Brading* is bound for Pier Head, with the luggage vans marshalled nearest to the ships for speedy transfer of passenger cases and trunks. Note the covered footbridge and ornate signal bracket. (P. Hay collection)

55. By the branch standards, three bogie coaches was a long train. Here we see no. W13 *Carrisbrooke* passing the main line connection on the afternoon of 23rd July 1935. Additional telephone or telegraph circuits had been provided on metal extensions to the wooden arms. (S.W. Baker)

56. *Shanklin* simmers in the bay platform whilst a sea mist blows in on an autumn day in 1937. The expense of providing a catch point in the loop seems to have been offset by economy in the construction of the buffer stops. (S.W. Baker)

57. A charming study in branch line expectancy. The guard leans against the nameboard; the driver reclines in the cab; the loco enthusiast stands at ease and one can imagine a curlew calling in the reclaimed marshes behind the engine, as all await the arrival of the main line train from Ryde. The date passed by unrecorded. (R. Silsbury collection)

The 1908 map shows the limited length of both the goods yard and the branch carriage siding. WM refers to a weighing machine.

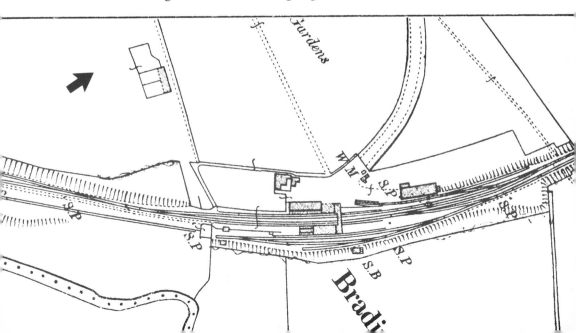

58. On 21st May 1956, no. W22 appropriately named *Brading* glides round the curve with its driver ready to surrender the single line token. The tiny goods yard might have grown had the coal seam discovered in Whitecliff Bay in the 1880s been more productive. The branch signals have gone and the rails lie rusty. (A.E. Bennett)

60. Electric sets often pass here, at the end of the double track section to Shanklin. The 13 elegant swan neck gas lamps survive in use in 1985 controlled by automatic time clocks, as the station is no longer staffed. We believe that Ilkley is the only other station on BR to have platforms gas lit. (J. Scrace)

59. A slightly different view from the foot-bridge nine years later shows the branch lifted and the goods siding overgrown. No. 16 *Ventnor* seems rather shabby but the flower beds are still cared for. The disused cement works is in the middle distance and St. Helens gasholder in the far distance. (E. Wilmshurst)

61. Looking north in 1985, the canopies look neglected but some restoration work was starting. A Youth Opportunities Programme involved renovating and reopening the waiting rooms and landscaping the area on the right. The signal box continues in use in its now rather remote position. (V. Mitchell)

63. A quarter of a mile along the branch was Brading Cement Works, which had provided the railway with an intermittent source of revenue, being active in late Victorian times and again between the wars. No. 14 *Fishbourne* is seen passing by the works sidings on 1st June 1953, with the small signal box in the distance. (P. Hay)

→

64. The sidings were used for the storage of redundant rolling stock. Some can be seen through the signal box windows, in this 1953 photograph. An account of the branch in 1948 read "an atmosphere of decay and inactivity pervades the surroundings of the railway". (J.H. Aston)

→

62. The origin of the former station master's house is evident in the monogram. In the porch is Ron Russell, the IOW Area Inspector for BR from 1960 until 1966. The house was provided with the job but when the post ceased to exist, he bought the dwelling. (V. Mitchell)

# THE BEMBRIDGE BRANCH

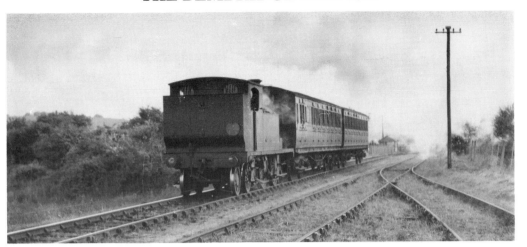

RAILWAY EXECUTIVE
SHOOTING, FISHING AND
EGGING PROHIBITED.

BY ORDER.

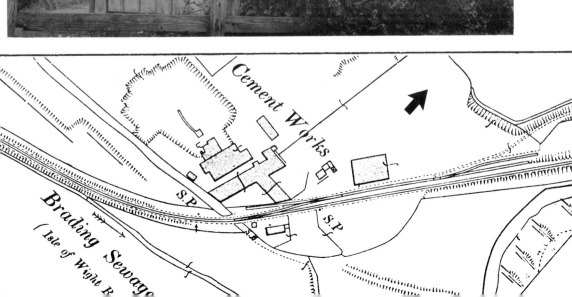

# St. HELENS

As part of the reclamation scheme, quays were constructed on the northern shore of Brading Harbour at St. Helens. The Brading Harbour Improvement and Railway Company also constructed the branch line and laid out sidings on the quays, traffic being worked by the IWR from the opening on 27th May 1882. At about that time the Isle of Wight Marine Transit Co. was formed and it bought (secondhand!) a small train ferry from the North British Railway in Scotland. The vessel, *P.S. Carrier*, operated in 1885-88 carrying goods wagons between St. Helens and Langston, near Hayling Island. A section of our *Branch Lines to Hayling* is devoted to a detailed description of this unusual paddle steamer together with the unique steam-propelled loading cradles.

The 1898 map shows the River Yar contained by embankments; controlled by sluices and crossed by the road and railway to Bembridge and also by the South Quay branch. Two tracks of the latter are shown terminating on the slipway where the *P.S. Carrier* had formerly berthed. The road crosses Brading Harbour on the sea wall and successive railway authorities collected tolls until the County Council acquired the road. The railway route to Bembridge was on a lower embankment on the reclaimed land. For many years a 2 ft gauge railway ran between the gas works and North Quay, crossing the road on the level. The wharves were rebuilt in 1932 but their use declined owing to improvements made to Medina Wharf.

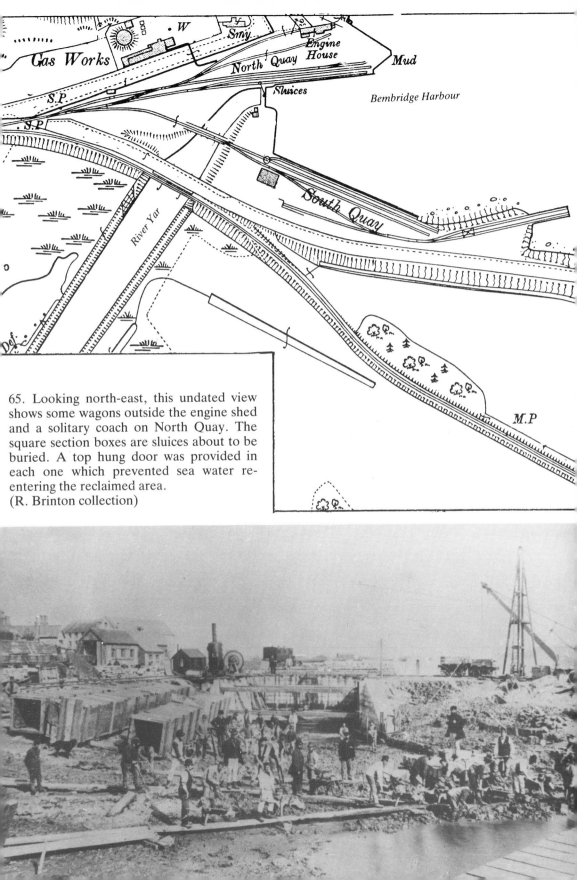

65. Looking north-east, this undated view shows some wagons outside the engine shed and a solitary coach on North Quay. The square section boxes are sluices about to be buried. A top hung door was provided in each one which prevented sea water re-entering the reclaimed area.
(R. Brinton collection)

66. Chaplin & Co were cartage agents to the LSWR in Portsmouth and had offices and a large storage shed on North Quay. The locomotive shed roof and water tank can be seen above the vans. (R. Brinton collection)

1884

| BRADING to BEMBRIDGE | WEEK DAYS. | | | | | | SUNDAYS. | | | | |
|---|---|---|---|---|---|---|---|---|---|---|---|
| | 1,2,P | 1 & 2 | 1 & 2 | 1 & 2 | 1 & 2 | 1 & 2 | 1,2,P | 1 & 2 | 1 & 2 | 1 & 2 | 1 & 2 |
| | a.m. | a.m. | p.m. | p.m. | p.m. | p.m. | p.m. | p.m. | p.m. | p.m. | p.m. |
| BRADING J. dep. | 8 37 | 10 52 | 1 41 | 3 40 | 5 51 | 8 16 | 1 3 | 2 10 | 3 10 | 4 37 | 8 57 |
| ST. HELEN'S arr. | 8 42 | 10 57 | 1 46 | 3 45 | 5 56 | 8 21 | 1 8 | 2 15 | 3 15 | 4 42 | 9 2 |
| BEMBRIDGE ,, | 8 47 | 11 2 | 1 51 | 3 50 | 6 1 | 8 26 | 1 13 | 2 20 | 3 20 | 4 47 | 9 7 |

| BEMBRDGE. to BRADING J. | WEEK DAYS. | | | | | | SUNDAYS. | | | | |
|---|---|---|---|---|---|---|---|---|---|---|---|
| | 1,2,P | 1 & 2 | 1 & 2 | 1 & 2 | 1 & 2 | 1 & 2 | 1,2,P | 1 & 2 | 1 & 2 | 1 & 2 | 1 & 2 |
| | a.m. | a.m. | p.m. | p.m. | p.m. | p.m. | p.m. | p.m. | p m. | p.m. | p.m. |
| BEMBRIDGE dp. | 8 13 | 10 35 | 1 12 | 3 20 | 5 35 | 7 48 | 12 47 | 1 55 | 2 55 | 4 20 | 7 37 |
| ST. HELEN'S ,, | 8 17 | 10 40 | 1 17 | 3 25 | 5 40 | 7 53 | 12 52 | 2 0 | 3 0 | 4 25 | 7 42 |
| BRADNG. J. arr. | 8 21 | 10 45 | 1 22 | 3 30 | 5 45 | 7 58 | 12 57 | 2 5 | 3 4 | 4 30 | 7 47 |

WEEKLY TOURIST TICKETS will be issued from APRIL 1st
to SEPTEMBER 30th, available for Seven Days' between all
Stations on the Isle of Wight and Brading Harbour Railways by all
Trains at the following Fares :—

First **7**s. **6**d. Class.    Second **5**s. **6**d. Class.

67. An April 1936 view shows push-pull working being undertaken by Terrier no. W13 *Carisbrooke* and two ex-LCDR coaches. The gas works and level crossing over the toll road are in the distance. (S.W. Baker)

**SOUTHERN RAILWAY.**

(9/23)                                                     787

TO

# ST. HELENS

68. Boilers were sent to Eastleigh for repair and an ex-IWR carriage truck was fitted with a well to house the firebox on the first stage of the boiler's journey from Ryde. Horse-drawn carriages had earlier been transported on such trucks and local legend recounts them being loaded complete onto the *P.S. Carrier*. (A.A.F. Bell)

Isle of Wight Ry
SPECIAL FARE
ST. HELENS
1 5.1     TO
SHANKLIN
Change at Brading
THIRD CLA?
Not Transferable. It
subject to the Compa.
Bye Laws & Published
Regulations.

508

70. W14 passes over the harbour junction bound for Bembridge. The photograph was taken from the level crossing on 1st June 1953. The station buildings, which were similar to those at Bembridge, have been converted into a fine residence. (P. Hay)

69. The engine shed ceased to be used as such in 1921 when the branch engine was supplied from Ryde each day. The building was subsequently used by the Permanent Way Department and was photographed in 1949. (A.A.F. Bell)

# BEMBRIDGE

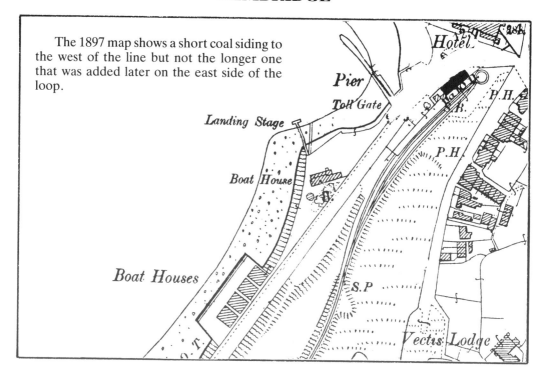

The 1897 map shows a short coal siding to the west of the line but not the longer one that was added later on the east side of the loop.

*Hotel*

*Pier*

*Toll Gate*

P.H.

*Landing Stage*

P.H.

*Boat House*

*Boat Houses*

S.P

*Vectis Lodge*

71. *Shanklin* stands at the terminus around the turn of the century. The semi-dormers gave status to the terminal buildings but were not provided at St. Helens. Note the solid or dumb buffers on the IWR wagon. (R.B. Owen collection)

72. A turntable of a mere 16'5" diameter was provided and was used as a sector plate to turn the engine about 20°. In cramped locations it took up less space than a point. (R. Silsbury collection)

73. The crew of W13 *Ryde* pose in front of a remarkable pair of secondhand coaches. The rear one was acquired from the Midland Railway by the IWCR and formed part of their second railmotor for a few years. The front one is the carriage portion of the railcar seen in picture no. 19. (J. Scrace collection)

74. The differing size of the dormer roofs is worthy of note, as is the bricklayer's attempt to incorporate the date in the end wall. The board at the back of the bus shows "To & From STATION". (J.G. Sturt)

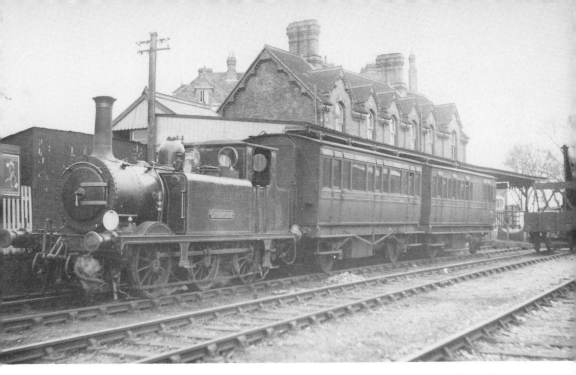

76. During the reconstruction, train services were maintained by no. W13 *Carisbrooke* (numbered 3 in picture no. 74!) with two ex- LCDR coaches fitted for push-pull working. The crane match wagon can be seen on the right. (S.W. Baker)

> Let us say frankly, lest we be accused of raising false hopes, that Bembridge will not suit every taste. It is a quiet, unconventional, old-world spot. " Minstrels " may pay occasional visits, but we have never seen them ; it has no band that we ever heard of ; and its residents and frequenters seem to have come to a tacit understanding that in the matter of dress " anything will do." The scenery is not sublime ; the smaller shops are still rather primitive ; and we are not even sure that the older cottages conform to the very latest requirements of civilization. But if you care for a place where the only noise is the laughter of children, where the only daylight occupations are yachting, golfing, bathing and fishing, and the evening occupations as nearly as possible *nil* ; where the only excitement of the day is the arrival of a railway train, then Bembridge is not likely to disappoint.

1928 Guide Book.

75. The scene on 11th April 1936 during the replacement of the small turntable by one of 25 ft diameter, capable of taking on Adams class O2 tank engine. In those days of cheap labour, a hand-operated crane lifting 10 tons was not given a second thought. (S.W. Baker)

77. As the push-pull set approaches the terminus, we gain a glimpse of the covered coal staithes. It was the practice to propel coal wagons from St. Helens to Bembridge and so one wonders why a loop and turntable were required at all. (R. Silsbury collection)

78. No. 14 *Fishbourne*, like no. 13 before it, was the branch engine for many years. Points to look for – steam escaping from the Westinghouse indicating that the air cylinder on the tank top was being pressurised; first class compartments (remarkable for a 10 minute journey); the shunter's pole parked high to avoid stooping and the scotch block on the siding. (P. Hay)

79. No doubt the fireman was thinking of the merits of push-pull working whilst moving his 47-ton machine. Space precluded the provision of the usual ramp at the end of the platform, another unusual feature of this station. Both photographs were taken during the last summer of branch operation. (J.H. Aston)

SOUTHERN RAILWAY.

(9/23)                                    787

TO

BEMBRIDGE

# SANDOWN

80. The stylish station buildings housed the headquarters of the IOWR nearly to the end of its independent existence. Here we see a train Ventnor-bound, in Edwardian days, with the platform for Newport trains on the extreme left. The massive tree was soon to obscure the view from the signal box beyond and was felled. (R.B. Owen collection)

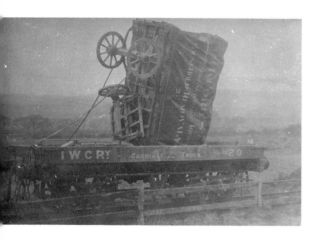

81. We feel that faded photographs are worth including if they are particularly interesting. Carriage trucks were sometimes used to convey other road vehicles – in this case with the disastrous effects of rough shunting. The location appears to be the brickworks siding, seen on the map in the divergence of the Newport and Ryde lines. (R. Brinton collection)

82. Another fine Edwardian photograph – the down platform with a profusion of posters and an unusual staff crossing facility, i.e. a missing brick and a projecting stone. (R.B. Owen collection)

The track layout changed little over the years, even when double track to Brading was brought into use in 1927. The angle of the railway boundary with Station Lane brought into being a curious house, seen as a triangle on this 1908 map and worth a glance when next leaving the station.

Sandown Junction

83. In this 1926 view we can enjoy the fine detail of the platform canopies and appreciate the value of a tall signal box on a curved station. The rear of a Newport train can be seen at platform 3. (K. Nunn/LCGB)

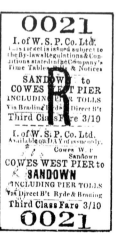

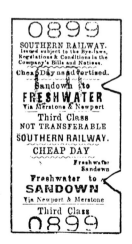

85. Now we see the 1.29 departure for Ryde Pier Head, which started at Sandown and only stopped at Brading. Note the small platform for van traffic and the diamond crossover. The latter was a device used at most of the Meon Valley stations (see our *Branch Lines to Alton*) and reduced the length of goods yards. (P. Hay)

84. The next four photographs, taken on Saturday 17th September 1955, give an impression of high level of activity over a period of 45 minutes, although the crowds had thinned out at that end of the season. At 1.20 pm *Calbourne* rumbles in from Ventnor with a train composed of alternating SECR and LBSCR coaches. The Cowes via Newport train is awaiting connection in the background. (P. Hay)

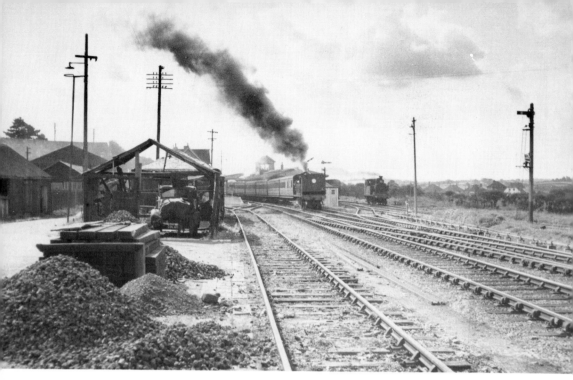

86. 1.40 pm. The firebox door was doubtless rattling as no. W24 pulled away with the 1.20 pm Ventnor to Ryde Pier Head. On the right, W30 runs round its train, ready to leave at 2.08 pm for Newport and Cowes. Domestic coal formed a large part of local freight traffic. (P. Hay)

S. & I. of W. S. P. Co. Ltd.
& SOUTHERN RAILWAY Co.

**SOUTHAMPTON**
TO
**SANDOWN**
Via Cowes
SINGLE JOURNEY
3rd. CLASS FARE
Including ALL Pier Tolls
**FOR CONDITIONS SEE BACK**

88. Returning holiday makers often queued four deep in the street in the 1950 s. By the time this photograph was taken in 1964, the crowds were more easily handled. The SR modernised the station in 1939 and provided the concrete name board and octagonal lampshades. (E. Wilshurst)

87. At 2.03 pm, no. W14 is seen arriving with the 1.42 from Ryde, passing the goods yard crane and the diverging Newport line. On summer Saturdays, this train did not stop at Brading. (P. Hay)

89. Only eight weeks before retirement, *Merstone* stands grimy and devoid of nameplates. It is dribbling injector water defiantly onto the new conductor rail and blowing steam at non-existent passengers, although even now the platform is often swarming with school children. Over 200 travel daily from Brading alone to the nearby County Secondary School. (J.A.M. Vaughan)

London Brighton and South Coast Railway.

Arundel to

# Sandown

90. After electrification, the loop became an engineers siding and the junction area was used for storage of permanent way materials. Although a recent photograph, the entire stock has been preserved on the Isle of Wight Steam Railway. Hunslet class O5 no. 97803 was formerly shunter no. D2554 at Harwich Parkeston Quay and was replaced by a class O3 in 1984. In the foreground is the iron roof of the subway complete with glass block skylight. (J.A.M. Vaughan)

# SHANKLIN

91. The hand written note on the original print reads "The first train to officially enter Shanklin station in 1864." The station was to remain a terminus for two years and to revert to that status a century later. Look at the uniforms in detail and the goods shed in the distance. (R. Brinton collection)

92. It was not long before the station developed an acne of enamelled advertisements. The loop is longer than in the previous photograph but the second platform had not yet been built. (R. Brinton collection)

An interesting feature of the 1908 map is the coal chute from the short siding down the side of the embankment directly into the gas works.

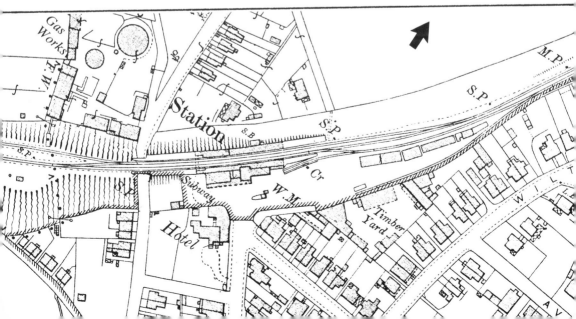

93. Cabs and carriers stand where the horse-drawn coach to Ventnor used to wait when Shanklin was first a terminus. The roof of part of the station extension is finished with pierced ornamental ridge tiles. (R.B. Owen collection)

95. During shunting procedures on 27th August 1962, brake van no. 56049 passed through the buffer stops at the end of the long siding to the north of the station. As this was at a higher level than the running line the van fell on its side. Ryde breakdown crane moved the victim to one side, where it was dissected and destroyed. (A.E. Bennett)

94. IWR locomotive *Sandown* awaiting departure for Ryde whilst the staff pose for photography around the turn of the century and station painting is in progress. (Lens of Sutton)

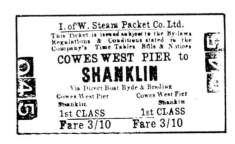

I. of W. Steam Packet Co. Ltd.
This Ticket is issued subject to the By-laws Regulations & Conditions stated in the Company's Time Tables Bills & Notices
COWES WEST PIER to
**SHANKLIN**
Via Direct Boat Ryde & Brading
Cowes West Pier          Cowes West Pier
Shanklin                      Shanklin
1st CLASS                 1st CLASS
Fare 3/10              Fare 3/10

97. Crowds of passengers disgorge from a southbound train on 22nd August 1964 whilst an up train stands in the opposite platform. Half way down the signal post is a small "calling on" signal, which allowed locomotives of terminating trains to pull forward before running round. (E. Wilmshurst)

←

96. The position of the signal box is shown on the map as SB. Signalmen had to work with great precision and promptness to keep the single lines working to schedule. (A.A.F. Bell)

→

98. Both platforms were electrified initially but with revised services only one was required. The single line now terminates at the end of the platform, as the road bridge has been removed. The platform was reduced in length at the southern end, the corresponding northern extension being visible in this 1985 view. There is still opportunity to admire the fine tracery of the canopy brackets. (C. Hall)

Way out

# WROXALL

99. The station looks unfamiliar without a canopy and second platform. The latter was added in 1925 when the passing loop was installed. On the right is the Wroxall Hotel, with the refreshment room door conveniently opening direct onto the platform. (R.B. Owen collection)

The 1908 map shows up and down sidings, the latter serving the bacon factory. Access to this siding was from the new loop after 1925.

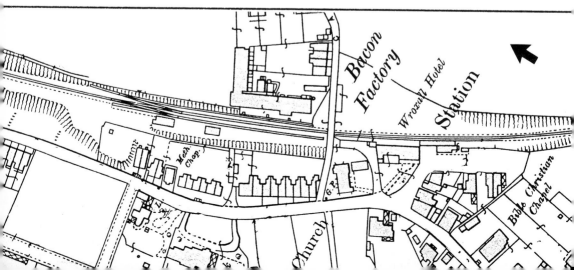

100. In bygone days, oil lamps were provided at this station for each compartment of southbound trains, before they entered the ¾-mile long tunnel to Ventnor. The ex-Metropolitan Railway coaches seen here were electrically lit from the ex-LSWR generator van at the rear. Many of these coaches survive as beach chalets on The Duver at St. Helens. (Lens of Sutton)

101. Other SR additions were the signal box on the platform; the footbridge and a roof on the Gents, on the left. Wroxall is situated in a hollow on the north side of the Downs and so mist is not unusual – even in June 1963, when this photograph was taken. (P. Hay)

102.  The rhythmic beating of crickets in the long grass of August 1965 competes with the rhythmic beating of the Westinghouse air pump to create a joyful concert for the ears of lovers of steam and countryside. An additional artistic touch is the signal post finial silhouetted against the steam from no. 35. (E. Wilmshurst)

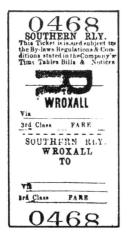

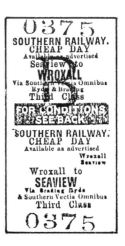

## SOUTHERN RAILWAY.

(3/25)

Stock
787

TO

# WROXALL

103. A 1965 view of the exterior shows the need for a nameboard to announce that the building is not just a bungalow. The timber structure of Ryde St. John's Road was similarly covered with stucco. (E. Wilmshurst)

104. The fine southward panorama from the footbridge has been lost for ever. This sentimental attitude is nothing compared with the loss of cash suffered by the traders and hoteliers of Ventnor with the closure of the line only weeks after this photograph was taken on 30th September 1965. (J.A.M. Vaughan)

105. By 1969, the platform side of the hotel gave the impression that the public bar was rather private. (J.A.M. Vaughan)

106. The northern end of the tunnel through St. Boniface Down was at the summit of the line, which rose at 1 in 173 from Ventnor and at 1 in 88 from Wroxall. No. 24 *Calbourne*, now preserved at Haven Street, is seen re-entering daylight on 14th July 1949. The Up. distant signal post's finial is in the foreground. (J.D. Knight)

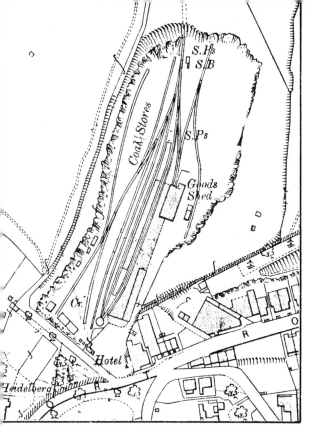

# VENTNOR

The 1908 map shows the maximum number of lines that were ever provided within the restricted site.

107. The station was constructed in a chalk quarry and extensive quarrying continued after services commenced as is evident when comparing this view with later ones. Note the birdcage guard's lookouts at each end of the train and also the incomplete station roof. (R. Brinton collection)

108. This photograph from about 1870 is well worth examining with a magnifying glass. A splendid hand cart is in the foreground, close to the stockaded turntable. (P. Primmer collection)

109. The sheltered coal stage opposite the signal box was eventually made redundant by fitting larger coal bunkers to the O2 class locomotives. The signals at the tunnel mouth were often difficult to see due to smoke in the tunnel and were replaced by colour light signals fixed to the tunnel wall. (R.B. Owen collection)

110. A view from the cliff top reveals the glass roof between the station buildings and the platform canopy; also the different profiles of the other canopies and some IWR wagons. (Lens of Sutton)

112. The now famous *Calbourne* awaits to leave with the 2.10 pm departure on 27th July 1926. The IWR were negotiating with the LSWR for the purchase of this engine, long before the SR was formed. The island platform was an operational nuisance as it was not wide enough to accept a footbridge and so portable platform level bridges were used. (K. Nunn/LCGB)

111. As at Bembridge, the turntable did not completely turn the locomotives as there was no turntable at the other end of the journey. The SR found that there was sufficient room to replace it with a point. *Ventnor* was the fourth Beyer Peacock acquired by the IWR and it survived until 1925.
(R.B. Owen collection)

←

113. The goods shed and the first Ryde engine shed were built from stone excavated during the tunnel construction. Another incidental benefit from its construction was the discovery of springs which still contribute to the town's water supply. A covered footway can be seen from which the signalman handed the single line tokens to the locomotive crew. (A.A.F. Bell)

114. The signal box diagram, as seen in 1963, makes an interesting comparison with the 1908 map. The cloth on the lever was held against the handle to prevent the salt from sweaty hands rusting it. (A.A.F. Bell)

115. A welcome sign to many anxious passengers on the Island's non-corridor trains. Although many ex-main line coaches were formerly fitted with toilets, these were converted to rather odd-shaped passenger compartments. The glazed roof gave an airy feeling on arrival at the Island's most southerly and sunny resort. (A.A.F. Bell)

116. This photograph, taken in 1963, is included to emphasise the fact that the railways always carried vast quantities of domestic coal, in addition to coal for their own locomotives and the various gasworks. There can have been few stations where the coal merchants were accommodated in caves! They also made good air raid shelters during World War II. (A.A.F. Bell)

117. The 6.20 departure on 21st June 1963 illustrates another problem of working the island platform – the rear coach is off the end of it. The sea is in the distance and 276ft lower than the station, which prompted a proposal for a funicular railway to the shore. (J. Scrace)

118. For cliff-loving birds, the area was a sheltered paradise and they added another rural dimension to the special sounds of this railway outpost. Spare coaches were often kept amongst the coal wagons, to strengthen up trains when necessary. Here we see no. 22 about to run round its train on 19th March 1966. (E. Wilmshurst)